AVOID HARD WORK!

...AND OTHER ENCOURAGING MATHEMATICAL PROBLEM-SOLVING TIPS FOR THE YOUNG, THE VERY YOUNG, AND THE YOUNG AT HEART

BY MARIA DROUJKOVA, JAMES TANTON, AND YELENA MCMANAMAN

IS WHAT YOU MAKE OF IT!

Natural Math

ISBN: 978-1-945899-01-0
Library of Congress Control Number: 2016913242

Text: Maria Droujkova, James Tanton, Yelena McManaman
Editing: Carol Cross, Karla Lant
Illustrations: Ever Salazar
Cover: Mark Gonya
Layout: Jana Rade

Published by Delta Stream Media, an imprint of Natural Math
309 Silvercliff Trail, Cary, NC, USA

Natural Math

This book came about thanks to parents, teachers, and math circle leaders who tested the activities, gave feedback, and crowdfunded the production of the book. Thank you for your support!

Anonymous
Adrian Smith
Aleksandra Ravas
Alexander Bogomolny
Alexandr Rozenfeld
Alexandra Otto
Alfreda Poteat
Algot Runeman
Alison Hansel
Amanda Gilbert
Amie Albrecht
Amy Sinclair
Andrew Kaplan
Andrius Kulikauskas
Anna
Anna Matson
Arashk Hamidi
Arun
B. & G. Etin
Ben North
Benji Jasik
Bertrand Behm
Bill Blaskopf
Bob Klein
Bradley Staeben
Burke Family
Cameron Goble
Cat Mikkelsen
Catherine Morrison
Charles H. Settles
Christopher
CY Goh

Cyrus & Dilan Muqbil
Dan Finkel
Dani Novak
Daniela Lawlor
Daria Korneeva
Denise Gaskins
Devin
Dr. Brandy
E. Coleman
Elena Tselishcheva
Elena Koldertsova
Elicia Moody
Elizabeth J. van Vuuren
Elizabeth Richards
Enric Margall
ESM
Evgenia Gavryuchkov
Fee Kapadia
Gabriella Pinter
Garrett Casey
Hannah & Aidan Fisk
Heather Sarik
Heather Heon
Irina Lvovsky
Jan Šedo
Japheth Wood
Jarkko Laine
Jason Boudi
Jason Gottfried
Jeanette Parry
Jelena Pavicevic
Jennifer Doggett

Jim Burtoft
John Nolan
John Strohm
Jolene Gleason
Jonathan Halabi
Jorie Walker
Joseph Austin
Jovan Knezevic
Julia Brodsky
Julie Moronuki
Julio Leyva
June Turner
Karen Snowball
Kathy Cordeiro
Kathy Howe
Kelli Warner & Carlos Cruz Montaño
Kennedys
Kenny Felder
Kirby Urner
Lana Boots
Lana Shyshova
Laura Ellen Jones
Laura Holte
Lauren Sieg
Leanne Paulin
Lee Ann Dietz
Lena Schuck
Lhianna Bodiford
Liza Shevyakhova
Marina Sokolsky
Mark McCarthy

Table of Contents

Introduction

PLAYFUL MATH WITH JAMES TANTON

James Tanton's mathematics education work is futuristic. To paraphrase the saying from science fiction, his teaching and learning techniques are so advanced they are indistinguishable from magic. Working with Dr. T, children feel like problem-solving superheroes. They become capable of glorious feats in rather advanced mathematics. Some time ago James created ten essays summarizing ten key techniques his students learn. The Natural Math team asked James to join them in adapting his magic for the younger crowd, and here it is.

THE ESSAYS

This is a companion piece to a set of essays on mathematics problem-solving. There are ten MAA *American Mathematics Competitions Curriculum Inspiration* pieces, each focusing on a particular strategy or mind-set. The focus of these essays is on the rekindling of the joyful intellectual play we all loved as youngsters, this time in the context of upper-level mathematics. The essays appear at maa.org/ci

In this book we show how the same ten key techniques can be of relevance and help to the very young. Each technique comes with a query to think about. As the adult leader, you supply the helpful scaffolding while students construct their solutions. In other words, techniques are not only for you to read, but also for you to then translate for the children!

Do also read the ten essays. Although more sophisticated in their mathematics, they will give you a good sense of each tactic discussed. You will be able to adapt the message of the strategy to the mathematics you are studying with young children.

A WORD ON WORDS

The term **problem-solving** sounds scary. Who wants problems? Why do we want to subject ourselves and youngsters to problems?

The word *problem* comes from the word *probe*, meaning *inquiry*. Inquiry is a much friendlier idea. Rather than attack a problem that has been given to us, let us accept an invitation to inquire into and to explore an interesting opportunity. Even toddlers can excel at inquiring, exploring, and investigating the world around them.

Will this curiosity extend to math learning? Yes, as long as the inquiries remain playful! For example, children naturally like to count things – both forward and backward. (*Is the number of steps up a staircase the same as the number of steps down? Shall we check?*) They love to arrange things in order of size. (*Could a container that holds more water than a pot still fit inside the pot?*) They love to trace paths on pavers or grids of stepping stones. (*Is it possible to reach the final paver stepping only on every second one? Every third one? Every fourth? Which numbers are "magic" in this way for this garden walkway?*) Youngsters naturally love to do mathematics!

CELEBRATE YOUR INNER TODDLER

Here are six main principles of adapting activities for the youngest explorers:

- Use large objects and gross motor skills.
- Keep the numbers small.
- Use sets of objects to show numbers.
- Pretend-play with characters that matter to your child.
- Tell a story of what's going on in the problem and why.
- Make and remix puzzles together with the child.

You can use these same tools to adapt other mathematics for the youngest learners.

Some older children and even grown-ups love these adaptations. Should you worry if this describes you or your older child? Nope! Celebrate your inner toddler!

These younger versions of the puzzles aren't much easier, mathematically speaking, but the presentation is more accessible. Art, storytelling, and pretend-play know no age. You or your older kids may like the "land and water" version of the *Lines and Dots* puzzle in Technique 8 because it has storytelling complexity and context. Maybe that's what you seek in your math.

You may wonder, "How can I help my child if I can't solve some of these problems myself?" Everything we recommend for children will help you, as well. Look at this situation as an opportunity to practice the ten problem solving techniques together with your child! Abandon the role of an instructor and instead be your child's playmate. Your child gives you a second chance in life - a chance to heal your relationship with math. Toddlers, who never suffer from math anxiety, can be your role models.

Rediscover the delight of open inquiry and curiosity! Mess around and enjoy the process – that's what toddlers do when they play. Even when you don't finish the problem, you and your kid are spending quality time with math, and learning the techniques. Give yourself the gift of time. There is no rush. Toddlers don't care about timed exercises.

Open up to the world. Ask your friends and their kids about a puzzle that you seem to be stuck on, or post it to social networks like Twitter or Facebook, or use the forum at ask.NaturalMath.com/community/. Like a toddler who brings the beloved toy everywhere, bring your math with you wherever you go!

My Dream

We asked hundreds of parents and teachers: "When it comes to children and mathematics, what are your dreams?" Here is what they told us.

For our children, we dream that mathematics...

... makes sense
... is more than just arithmetic
... is joyous
... makes them strong
... is meaningful
... is creative
... is full of fascinating questions
... opens up many paths to solutions
... is friendly
... solves big problems and makes the world better
... is a powerful tool they can master
... is beautiful
... lets them learn in their own ways
... is connected to their lives
... asks "why" and not just "how"
... opens the world

Teaching Techniques

These teaching techniques are companions to the problem-solving techniques. They will help you to support mathematical play, inquiry, and exploration. Do try this at home!

1. Write down clever, kind, silly, wise, funny, curious, inspiring, exciting things kids say as they try to solve problems. Create memories!

2. Present a problem you like, but you are sure is too advanced for the child. Do not hope for an answer, but give the child a chance to probe, ask questions, and explore. Demonstrate that it's perfectly okay if a problem is not solved for months or even years.

3. Collect and exhibit pictures, quotes, and other tidbits your child liked on a bulletin board. Kids will be reminded to review math through their favorite pieces, building up understanding and joy.

4. Revisit problems that were interesting to the child. You can solve the same problem again a few months later, remix it yourself, or find a similar problem.

5. Capture your work toward the solution in simple cartoons or photos of your setups, and display on a bulletin board.

6. Keep baskets of puzzles and manipulatives, or individual math toys and books, where the child can see and reach them.

7. Invite your child to explain how to solve a problem to a friend or a younger kid. Explaining to an adult might feel like being tested.

8. Always leave room for exploration: extra space and time. Think of mathematics as a road trip. You have the directions, but might want to try a scenic route, visit a roadside attraction, take an unexpected detour, or stay for a picnic.

9. If you are tempted to judge the child's answer wrong and want to start correcting, first ask the simple "why?" question. Most of the time kids have meaningful reasons behind their strange answers. Discussing children's "whys" will teach them more math than explaining your "hows."

10. Go beyond the original problem or even leave it behind. Working toward a solution you might discover other related problems that pique your curiosity. Go for them!

Questions and Answers #1

Q: HOW OLD SHOULD MY CHILD BE TO WORK ON THESE PROBLEMS?

A: We have adapted the problems for two levels: approximately 3-5 year-olds and 6-8 year-olds. Some families modified the problems for younger toddlers, and many report that older children, teens, and of course parents enjoyed using these materials. A good problem, like a good story, stretches **across ages**. The essays mentioned in the book were originally aimed at teens. You can find these essays and examples of how different families use the materials and contribute your own questions and examples at our forum.

Q: DOES MY CHILD NEED TO KNOW HOW TO COUNT, ADD/SUBTRACT, OR MULTIPLY IN ORDER TO WORK ON THESE PROBLEMS?

A: Not at all. **There are no prerequisites**. We will show you how to adjust each activity so that even very young children can participate and enjoy it.

Q: IS THERE AN APP FOR THIS? CAN I HELP MY CHILD ACQUIRE PROBLEM-SOLVING SKILLS WITH COMPUTER GAMES OR APPS?

A: Problem-solving is about finding your own paths, and creating your own problems and solutions. Therefore, **the best computer activities for problem-solving are programming, modeling, and design,** in which you build something of your own. There are several good tools for young children to learn programming, such as Scratch from MIT. For modeling, use computer art programs, Minecraft or LEGO software, and math tools like GeoGebra. And for design, use computers to draft and create what your child loves: sewing patterns, book illustrations, boats or spaceships, new species of animals, comics and stories, or whatever else interests your child. Most designers, makers, and creators use computers these days, and many make child-friendly versions of their tools for the next generation.

Q: I KNOW THAT WHEN IT COMES TO CHILDREN, I NEED TO EXPECT THE UNEXPECTED. HOW CAN I DO IT WITH MATH?

A: Be prepared to abandon the plan. Learn now how to ask probing questions, listen attentively, and accept what you hear. **Stay tuned to the children** to notice their change in attitude: boredom, frustration, anxiety, tiredness, or lack of understanding. Do the improv exercise called YES, and... Put up the giant YES on the table or the wall to remind you. Whatever it is the child says or does, (1) *say* yes to it (2) *accept* that it means something (3) *brainstorm* what you can add to the meaning. Maybe your child's claim that 2+2 = 1 is an analogy, or a math joke, or a novel way to count. Exploring jokes, analogies, or funky counting will be more fun and will teach more math than the simple-minded, generic claim, "You are wrong."

Also, be prepared to change topics completely! Don't force a problem or an activity if the mood of the room, the "feeling in the air," just isn't right. Always keep a few extra activities ready, in case the original plan does not work. And make it clear, in a fun way, that you are changing topics, so that children learn this technique from you. You can always return to the original challenge at another time.

Q: HOW DO I KEEP CHILDREN EXCITED ABOUT DOING MATH? HOW DO I STAY ENTHUSIASTIC WHILE HELPING MY CHILD LEARN MATH?

A: Let the child do the teaching, so you are surprised and excited by the unexpected. Suggest they re-design math problems and teach them to you or other children or adults. Record their lessons and play them back to the child. Or take pictures of your children teaching and show them the pictures. Seek exciting math media, such as stories, videos, posters, or art, and share what you like with your child.

Q: WHAT CONCEPTS/SKILLS ARE IMPORTANT IN MATH EDUCATION AND WHICH ONES ARE NICE, BUT NOT NECESSARY?

A: There are many lists of mathematical practices, values, and dispositions. Everyone agrees that **noticing patterns** is what mathematics is really all about. And then come the questions: Are these patterns valid? Are they sure to keep working - forever? How can I test this? How can I know? Here is one of the recent lists, from a US document called *Common Core*.

1. Make sense of problems and persevere in solving them.
2. Reason abstractly and quantitatively.
3. Construct viable arguments and critique the reasoning of others.
4. Model with mathematics.
5. Use appropriate tools strategically.
6. Attend to precision.
7. Look for and make use of structure.
8. Look for and express regularity in repeated reasoning.

Half of the items are really about patterns (2, 4, 7, and 8). For example, abstract reasoning means seeing general patterns behind particular examples.

Q: IT IS EASY FOR ME TO TEACH LITERATURE, HISTORY, AND ART THROUGH STORIES. CAN I TEACH MATH THROUGH STORIES? HOW?

A: Read other people's math stories, such as *Alice in Wonderland* or *The Cat in Numberland*. Invite children to create their own stories about math - in words, or in pictures, or by pretend-play with action figures and toy animals. Children often like to be heroes in the stories - make it happen! **Only put math into stories with good reasons intrinsic to your story's world**. A hero may count friends and enemies, or prepare enough supplies for a quest. No hero ever wonders, out of the blue, what you get if you add two horses and three horses.

Recount your personal stories too. What was the first mathematical activity you ever remember doing? Did you know it was mathematics at the time? Ask your friends and colleagues about their first encounters - before schooling! - with mathematics. People often have delightful first stories.

Q: CAN A PERSON WHO IS NOT FLUENT IN MATH CALCULATIONS BE OTHERWISE A CONFIDENT AND RELAXED MATH LEARNER?

A: Yes. Even mathematicians can be this way. You do need to be fluent in patterns, formulas, and concepts. Some mathematicians might say that actual computation is secondary to the mathematics at hand; getting a numerical answer in the end is just a final detail. It is the "whys" and the "what ifs" over the "whats" that excite mathematicians!

Q: HOW DO I HELP CHILDREN GAIN CONFIDENCE IN SOLVING MATH PROBLEMS?

A: **Make it social**. For a child, working one-on-one with an adult can be intimidating, but when kids talk about a problem with friends, they may become more confident. Also, encourage children to make up their own puzzles and problems and pose them for adults and other children to solve. This maker stance produces confidence. Problem-solving is like research or exploration: there are a lot of blind valleys! **Make sure being stuck, trying wrong methods, and making mistakes is the norm in your daily math life**. Be especially careful with girls, because they are more socially responsible and thus more hesitant to do wild experiments or to give wrong answers. But it's okay to try and try again.

Validate any mathematical comment, even if it looks wildly "incorrect." At the very least, say: "Oh, what an interesting idea! That makes me think that maybe if we tried…" This way you give a nudge to the conversation, and also illustrate how all ideas, even wild ones, can inspire new routes of thought.

Q: HOW CAN I LEARN TO TAKE A COMPLEX MATH CONCEPT AND MAKE IT APPROACHABLE AND EASIER TO UNDERSTAND FOR CHILDREN WITH DIFFERENT LEARNING STYLES?

A: Making complex ideas accessible isn't easy. You can read popular books, magazines, and blogs about math and science to see how journalists do it. Here are a few techniques for making concepts approachable:

- Find a deep story, even drama, of why people of the world care about the concept.
- Arrange hands-on explorations: model the concept with objects kids can touch, or virtual objects and manipulatives.
- Go on a scavenger hunt for the concept in your daily life, so you can relate to it.
- Read the topic, and then try to describe it to yourself without using any of the specialised jargon. Or draw a wordless cartoon that captures the theme of the topic. Ask: What is the question really about? What is the issue being explored here? Why should anyone care about this? If you have the answer to the last question, then you have likely found the entry point to the concept!

Q: HOW CAN I HELP MY CHILD TO EXPERIENCE MATHEMATICS AS A BEAUTIFUL, USEFUL, AND CREATIVE ENDEAVOR?

A: The key question here is whether you can spend at least an hour or two a week doing real mathematics with your child. In some sci-fi universes, you can upload memories into your brain. But here, experiences equal time. The good news is that you can start casually. You can dedicate a quiet family evening, or a weekend park playdate with friends, and play with real mathematics. You can get a couple of like-minded friends together into an informal Math Circle that meets once a week or once a month.

You need to make math the natural human organic endeavor it is. Give it the space and freedom to be play - joyful intellectual play. Tell the human story of the subject.

A: If you feel like you are learning a lot about this level of mathematics, your role with your children changes. As the teacher saying goes, you go from sage on the stage to **guide on the side**. Fortunately, this is a job promotion. The saying comes from the title of a popular article about good teaching practices. When you solve problems, imagine you and your children collaborating on a little research project:

	Adults	Children
Ideas	Write ideas down, sort and organize sets of examples, articulate knowledge	Generate diverse, creative, novel, unexpected ideas
Mathematics	Maintain consistency of patterns, systematically extend patterns with new examples	Open up and maintain free play, break patterns to create new patterns
Process	Organize activities, manage time and tasks, maintain group well-being, nurture	Sense poor management practices, quickly show when well-being is in danger ("the canary"), invoke empathy and joy
Applications	Connect ideas to many life experiences and examples	Connect ideas to unexpected examples, look at familiar things from new angles
Aesthetics	Appreciate order and systems	Appreciate storytelling, links to nature, and adventure

Each project member will contribute, and together, you will explore the problem. Check out the table of what adults and children typically do well in problem-solving. As you can see, kids and grown-ups make a dream team, because their skills are complementary.

TECHNIQUE 1

SUCCESSFUL FLAILING

This technique is all about brainstorming, experimenting, and exploring. Try this and that, discuss with different people, try different angles, use different representations. Successful flailing consists of open play, while keeping an eye on your mathematical goals.

 ## DR. T'S PROBLEM

This puzzle also appears in Without Words *by James Tanton, Tarquin Press, 2015.*

If this:

Then what happens here:

Manipulatives will help kids to see how adjacent gears turn. You might already have some LEGO gears or the ones from the Gears!Gears! set. Or you can take apart an old printer: a fun activity for young kids. You can also cut gears out of craft foam and cardboard, or make some on a 3D printer.

STEPS TO SOLUTION

1. React emotionally to the problem. Is the contraption exciting? Is it overwhelming? Will you get lost in all the cogs?

2. Some children like to talk first and then experiment. Others would rather jump in with hands-on play, and then discuss. Try switching 3 and 4 below to see what works for your child.

3. Discuss the problem. Help children make sense of the diagrams. Some questions to ask:
   - What is on the first diagram? (Some gears, lined up.)
   - What do you think this arrow means? (It probably means one of the gears is being turned in this direction.)

- Why would the last gear move? Does it move? (It looks like it does. Other gears spread the movement to it.)

4. Experiment. Use manipulatives to figure out what happens to adjacent gears when one is turned. Kids may answer with actions rather than words. Ideas to try:
   - How many directions can a gear turn? (Two.)
   - Do all gears in the contraption turn? (Yes, if they are connected to each other.)
   - Do all gears turn in the same direction? (No!)
   - If I put three gears in a row, can you predict which way the last gear will turn? How about four? (The first gear spins this way; the second, the opposite way; the third spins the same way as the first gear, etc.)
   - Is there any way to arrange the gears so they jam? (This is too fun to try, so we won't spoil it by giving away the answers.)
   - What if we do not interlock gears, but instead connect them with a belt or a rubber band? (Another "try and see" idea.)

What happens here:

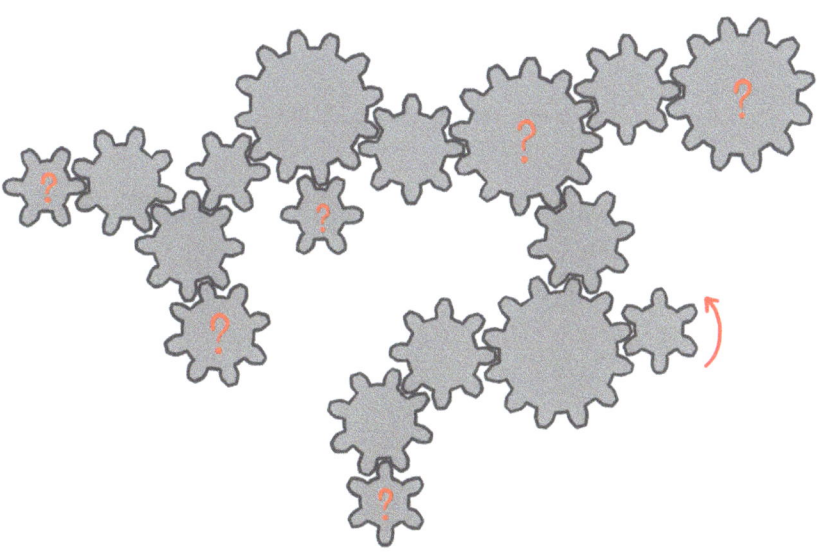

I TRIED THIS TECHNIQUE AND...

My child felt very discouraged, especially once someone else in the group came up with the right answer. How can I help her stay motivated?

Be a role-model for courage in problem-solving! This means, in part, sharing both your thoughts about how to solve a problem and the emotions the problem stirs in you. Speak your mind.

Invite kids to create their own problems. Faster, older, or more fluent kids can make up harder problems, or work on more problems. Since everybody is going at their own pace, there is less anxiety for all. Montessori environments use the same technique, with all children working on their own project until mastery, then moving on. Kids will also get creative with their problems: they will add stories, move to 3D, or add other manipulatives.

Keep the essence of the problem, but replace rotation with an up-and-down movement, and introduce some characters. Use a chair or a ladder, a string, and some toys. If you pull, will Hippopotamus go up or down? How about Cow? Encourage lots and lots of experimenting.

Toddler Time Techniques Used

- Use large objects and gross motor skills.
- Pretend-play with characters that matter to your child.

SCAVENGER HUNT

Look for other objects and activities in which something that moves in one direction causes something connected to move in the opposite direction. Check out the up and down sides of conveyor belts, investigate pulleys, play on see-saws, observe how revolving doors work as entrances and exits. Plus you finally get to solve the Egg Beater Mystery: how come the blades move in the opposite directions?

WHAT IS THE BIG IDEA HERE?

Math ideas explored in this game are:

- **Patterns** describe the mathematical essence of each situation. For example, gears in a row exhibit an alternating pattern of rotation (left-right-left-right) that is similar to the see-saw and pulley patterns (up-down-up-down).
- **Rules** describe how patterns work. For example, "alternate left and right" is a rule.
- **Parity** is the study of systems that come in one of two states (on/ off, up/down, left/right, even/odd, and so on).

 ## SAME TECHNIQUE - DIFFERENT PROBLEM

John and Hilde are at a library, looking through an exciting math book. Suddenly John exclaims: "Twenty pages have been ripped from this book!" Hilde replied: "I bet the sum of the missing page numbers is even." Her answer won't help John to finish his book, but is Hilde right?

Steps to Solution

You can discuss or experiment first, depending on what your kid prefers.

1. Have an emotional reaction to the problem. It's okay if Hilde bothers you a bit!

2. Discuss the problem. Help children make sense of it. Questions to ask:
   - What do we know about page numbers in books? Holding an actual book is helpful at this point. (Each page has a front and a back. Both fronts and backs of each page are numbered.)
   - So how many page numbers are missing? (More than twenty!)
   - How could Hilde know the sum of all the missing page numbers is even? This would be true if all the page numbers in the book were even. Are they? (No!)
   - Let's look at a book again. What do we notice about how each page is numbered? (There are even numbers on one side of book pages and odd number on the other sides. Hmm...)

3. Experiment. Ideas to try:
   - Take a small notebook or a stack of sticky notes and number the pages. Then take one page out. Is the sum of its front and back page numbers even? What if you take out two pages? Can you

predict whether the sum of page numbers for three pages will be even or odd? Four pages?

- If thus far you have been taking out consecutive pages, check what happens if you take out randomly-chosen pages.

Back to the problem. Is Hilde right?

TECHNIQUE 2

DO SOMETHING

Imagine you are on a rollercoaster at the very top of that first drop off. Looking around you see nothing but the sky in all directions. How you wish you didn't climb aboard! Facing a problem, mathematical or not, can sometimes feel very unnerving, like those seconds atop a rollercoaster ride. And just like the excitement you feel on a rollercoaster, the thrill of problem-solving is in moving closer to the solution - or somewhere!

If you get that "hanging in midair" feeling, do something about it. For example, you might sketch or role-play the problem, or guesstimate the solution. You might not know how to solve the problem (just like you don't know what twists and turns are coming up next on your ride), but knowing that you are doing something about it is a very empowering, exciting feeling.

 ## DR. T'S PROBLEM

A pin has two ends: one called a "head" and one called the "point."

Penny likes to arrange pins in loops. For example, here is a picture of six pins in a loop.

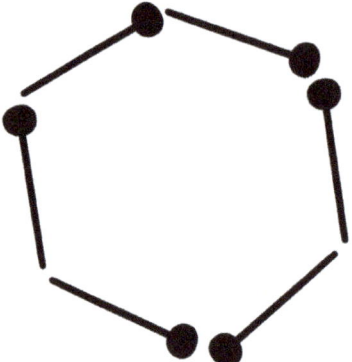

This picture has two places where a head and a head meet, two places where a point and a point meet, and two places where a point and a head meet.

One time Penny arranged ten pins in a loop. She told me that in her picture there were FIVE places where a head and a point met. Is she remembering correctly?

STEPS TO SOLUTION

1. React emotionally to the problem. Whether it makes you feel anxious, apprehensive, uncertain, curious, impatient, glad, excited, or anything else, it's okay.

2. Do something about it. Make the problem into a story. Children need a very strong reason for why something needs to be done (as do we all). It also has to be personal to them; that is, it must touch upon their interests, hobbies, or favorite objects. Therefore, you

might need to replace pins with dolls, mini-figures, stuffed animals, or finger puppets. If you are not using actual objects, but, say, stick figure drawings, a compelling story becomes even more important. If you have enough people present, you can even play out the story with kids instead of pins.

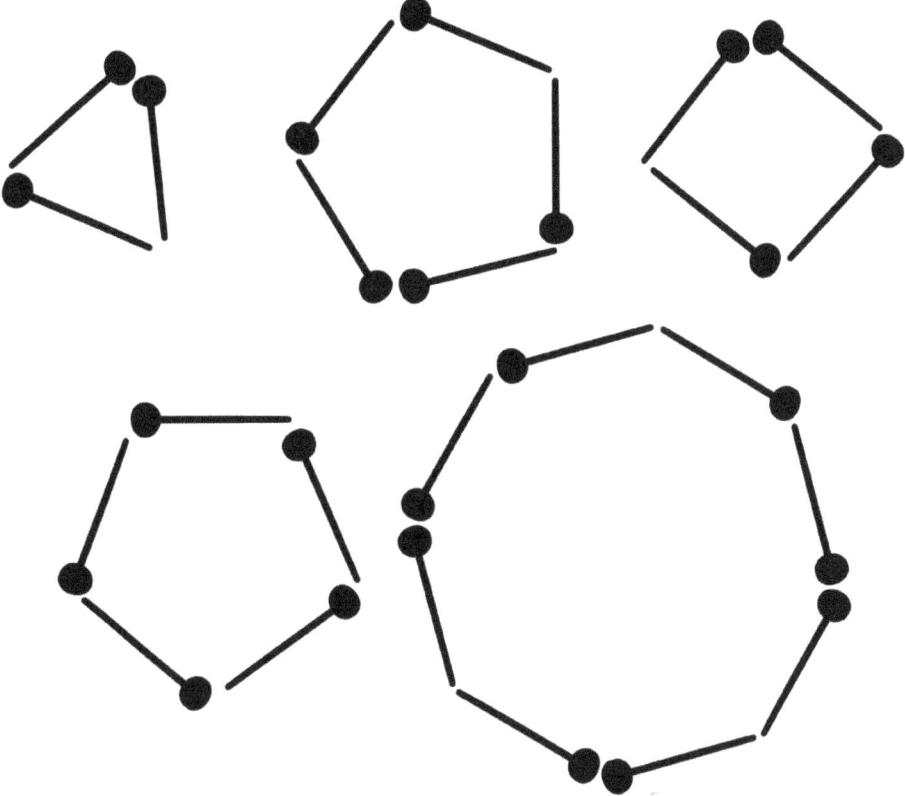

3. Experiment with arranging a small number of objects. Encourage the child to record her observations. See if something interesting emerges.
   - What do you notice about the count of head/head and point/ point pairs each time?
   - Can you predict head/head and point/point pairs for the next try?
   - Does the experiment confirm your hypothesis?

I TRIED THIS TECHNIQUE AND...

You can just "play through" some problems, but this one requires record-keeping. How can I introduce my child the idea of keeping records or using written symbols?

Be up front, but make a bit of a show of it: "Oh my, I am getting lost! I can't remember everything we're saying. What can we do?" The idea of recording ideas may come up, especially if there is a white board or poster paper for everyone to use together. Going from "point" to "p" comes naturally, but some kids will stick with drawings, not symbols. Support children in whatever record-keeping system they develop.

TODDLER TIME

Replace pins with favorite toys. Even if you are using familiar and well-loved toys, give your child plenty of play time with them before you begin. Tell a story, for example:

Penny played with six toys. They took a nap. Penny arranged them in a loop. When her "people" were head to head, she gave them a paper pillow to share. Penny decided she needed four pillows. Was she correct?

Invite your child to do something; move the toys around and see what happens.

Toddler Time Adaptations

- Use large objects and gross motor skills.
- Keep the numbers small.
- Pretend-play with characters that matter to your child.
- Tell the story of what's going on in your problem and why.

 SCAVENGER HUNT

Look for other objects and building materials that can be connected only in one direction such as LEGO blocks or extension cords. How many can you find that connect head-to-tail? Can you find any that connect head-to-head?

WHAT IS THE BIG IDEA HERE?

- **Graph theory** is the branch of mathematics that studies models linking pairs of objects.
- **Directed graph** is a model where links between objects have directions.

SAME TECHNIQUE - DIFFERENT PROBLEM

I am going to multiply the number two with itself 100 times:

2×2×2×2×...×2×2.

This will give me some huge number. What will be the final digit of that number?

STEPS TO SOLUTION

1. Have an emotional reaction to the problem.

2. Do something about it. Let's try using a calculator. Turn it on, punch in 2^{100}, look at the final digit. What happens? Some calculators will give an approximate answer, and some will produce gibberish. Hmm.

3. Experiment. Multiply twos:

   $2 \times 2 = 4$

   $2 \times 2 \times 2 = 8$

   $2 \times 2 \times 2 \times 2 = 16$

   $2 \times 2 \times 2 \times 2 \times 2 = 32$

   $2 \times 2 \times 2 \times 2 \times 2 \times 2 = 64$

   $2 \times 2 \times 2 \times 2 \times 2 \times 2 \times 2 = 128$

Okay, this is getting tedious. But can you see an emerging pattern? Can you predict what the next final digit would be? How about the one after next? Check to see if it works. If it does and you see the pattern, can you figure out the last digit for the 2^{100}? By the way, why does it work?

WISHFUL THINKING

"Imagine you met a fairy who could grant you
any wish. What would you ask for?"
"Ten thousand dollars!"
"Why not a million?"
"A million would not be realistic!"

This joke is funny because it's true: our wishful thinking is often inhibited. Even knowing fairies and math problems are made up, children might need help or "permission" to wish freely. It gets easier with practice.

DR. T'S PROBLEM

This problem is from *The Art and Craft of Problem Solving*, by Paul Zeitz.

Draw lines connecting A to A, B to B, and C to C in such a way that the lines do not cross.

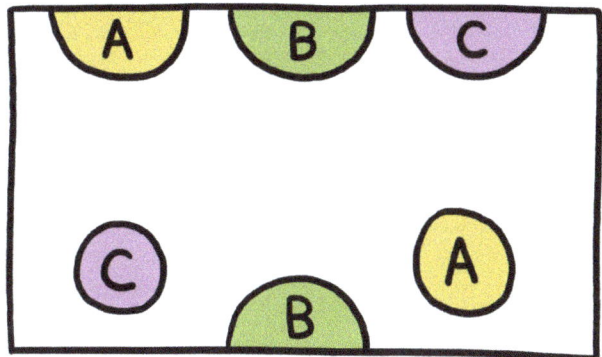

STEPS TO SOLUTION

1. React emotionally to the problem. Whether it makes you feel anxious, apprehensive, uncertain, curious, impatient, glad, excited, or anything else, it's okay.

2. Do something about it. It might be helpful to construct a model of this problem on poster-board with pairs of cardboard tiles labeled A, B, and C. Alternatively you might use playdough, or small toys and strings. If you have enough people, make a life-sized version of this puzzle with three pairs of kids standing by opposite walls.

3. Make a wish. I wish I could place tiles anywhere I wanted so the puzzle would be easier. I wish it was as easy as this diagram:

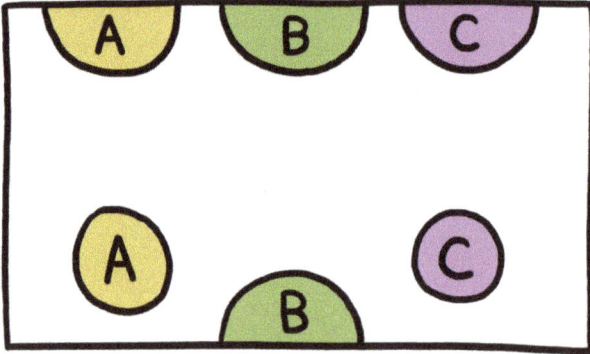

4. Experiment. Can we take the easy answer and "move it around" to get an answer to the original problem?

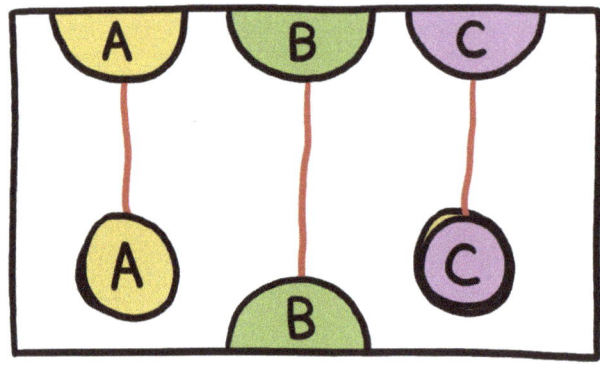

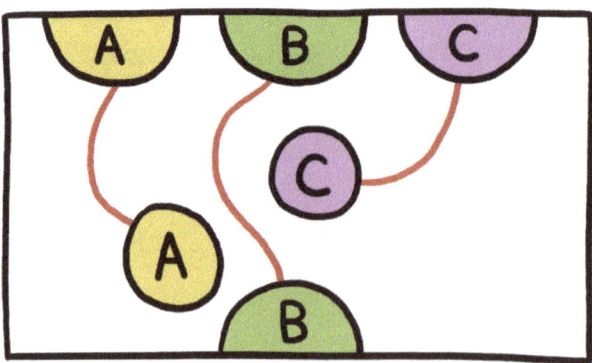

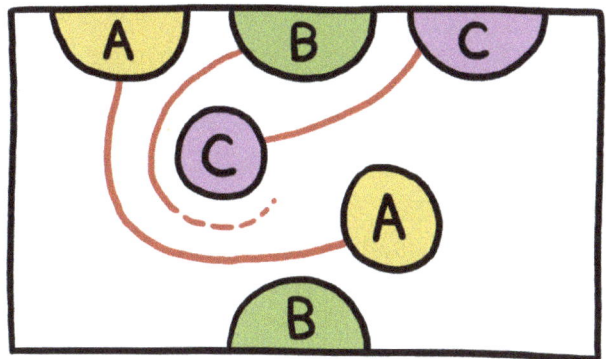

I TRIED THIS TECHNIQUE AND...

My child seemed more interested in the story I told her, and wanted to role-play it over and over. How can I make sure she pays more attention to the underlying math?

Although it might seem that role-playing children don't pay any attention to the math behind the story, they do care. They simply establish the plot, characters, and imaginary situation first. Their math is applied as they make animals safe from predators, keep dolls comfortable, and get the hero out of a trap. To encourage attention to mathematical structures, tell different stories where the same mathematics appears. Gently help your young applied mathematicians to notice the similarities in structures. This will lead children from particular examples to more general mathematical principles. Children find it surprising and profound when they can use the same math ideas to help completely different characters in different settings.

TODDLER TIME

Instead of lines and abstract circles with A-B-C and lines, use roads and houses of baby animals and their mommies. The roads between houses can't meet, because these animals aren't friendly with one another! For example, a dog can chase a cat when their roads meet. Kids may make roads meet just to see what happens! This is okay, because they are still exploring the situation. Would it be easier if animals could move their houses?

Toddler Time Adaptations

- Use large objects and gross motor skills.
- Pretend-play with characters that matter to your child.
- Tell a story of what's going on in the problem, and why.

SCAVENGER HUNT

Look for real life examples of roads or paths that do not cross. You might decide to take apart that old printer you kept, and look at the circuit boards. Going on a road trip? It's a perfect opportunity to check out highway interchanges.

WHAT IS THE BIG IDEA HERE?

Math ideas explored in this game are:

- **Graph theory** is the branch of mathematics that studies models linking pairs of objects.
- **The seven bridges of Konigsberg** is the famous 18th-century problem, now considered a part of graph theory.

SAME TECHNIQUE - DIFFERENT PROBLEM

Three sheep, Albert, Bilbert, and Cuthbert, are standing in a field, each happily munching away on grass. Is it possible for the distance between A and B, the distance between B and C, and the distance between A and C to be the same? How about four sheep standing in a field: Albert, Bilbert, Cuthbert, and Dilbert? Is it possible for the distances between pairs of them to always be the same?

Wishful thinking: I wish we weren't stuck to a flat field!

TECHNIQUE 4

THE POWER OF DRAWING

Before beginning to work on this problem, make sure your child understands how balance scale works. If you don't already have a balance scale, you can make one with a coat hanger, some string, and a couple of berry baskets. If you can find a see-saw at a playground, head outside for a large-scale, full-contact mathematical experience. Invite kids to explore first, playing with balance scales to compare weights of different toys, objects, and people.

DR. T'S PROBLEM

Three bags of apples and four single apples together weigh the same as one bag of apples and five single apples. If each bag contains the same number of apples, how many apples are in one bag?

STEPS TO SOLUTION

1. React emotionally to the problem.

2. Draw. This puzzle is so much easier to understand as a picture!

Let's draw a picture of what's going on.

3. Make a wish. Maybe this puzzle would be easier to solve if there were fewer apples? If we remove one apple from each side of the scale, will the scale remain balanced?

What if we remove one more apple from each side?

What if we remove a bag from each side? Will the scale remain balanced? Are we getting closer to figuring out how many apples are in one bag?

If your child is not certain about such questions while working with pictures, you will need to work more with a real balance scale, and then return to the problem.

I TRIED THIS TECHNIQUE AND...

My child just kept guessing the answer instead of trying to figure it out. How to deal with thoughtless guessing?

This happens a lot. Instead of fighting what kids want to do, turn this into a more thoughtful guessing game. Ask your child to check if the guess actually works. If it does, accept it. The process of checking can lead to interesting mathematical insights. Children also guesstimate to reduce their anxiety, which indeed helps a lot, as long as they also check the guesses.

Some kids can't or won't draw. My kid loves playing with balance scales, but does not want to use pencil and paper. What can I do?

What to do depends on why your kid does not want to draw. Some children are frustrated that they can't draw well, that they can't steady their hand, or that they can't draw particular shapes. To help with these issues, offer to hold your child's hand in yours as the child draws. Be gentle, and follow whenever the child's hand starts to lead. This helps with math learning, because the hand teaches the brain.

Your kid may not realize you can pretend-play with drawings, not just toys. Create a story that uses drawings and diagrams. The apple story's equation is $3x+4 = x+5$. Here's how one parent reimagined this story for his children.

"The giant has stolen the king's treasure. He escaped the King's land and voyaged to a desert island. You and your fellow brave knights chase the giant to the island. Once there, you hide behind a dune and observe the giant. Looks like he decided to bury the treasure! From the start of a path at the water's edge, the giant walked 3 giant steps and then, unwilling to go further, he told his regular-sized servant to take 2 regular sized steps and bury the treasure. The next day, the giant wanted to bury more treasure in exactly the same place. Setting off along the same path, he walked two giant steps and then the servant travelled the rest of the distance, which took him six regular sized steps. The giant and his servant returned to the ship and sailed off. Your job is to tell your fellow knights exactly where the treasure is in regular-sized steps."

The giant story's equation is $3x+2 = 2x+6$. Do you see why the parent changed the numbers in the giant story, compared to the apple story and its equation? Hint: giant steps are giant!

 ## TODDLER TIME

Turn it into a story of dolls and teddy bears (or your child's favorite toys) on a see-saw. Build a simple toy see-saw out of a board and a couple of building blocks and model the story. If you and your child are interested, you can explore the mechanics of the see-saw, such as the effects of unequal arms, which lead to more complex equations. You can use sticky notes or cards, which you draw and your toddler moves. See if your child would draw large pictures on a whiteboard, or on a sidewalk with chalk: large drawings are easier for toddlers to do.

Toddler Time Adaptations

- Use large objects and gross motor skills.
- Make and remix puzzles together with your child.
- Use sets of objects to show numbers.

SCAVENGER HUNT

Find contraptions that use balance beams, balance scales, or see-saws. For example, many mobile sculptures are a series of connected balance beams. Lifting cranes often contain counter-balances. A clothes hanger is a balance beam with a hook in the middle.

WHAT IS THE BIG IDEA HERE?

Math ideas explored in this game are:

- **Equation** is a statement that two entities are the same. The entities can be numbers, expressions, vectors, or even drawings and diagrams. In this problem, total weights are the same.
- **Unknowns** are parts of equations we don't know. Sometimes we can gather some knowledge about unknowns by examining equations. In this problem, bags of apples are unknown.
- **Equivalent equations** are true for the same values of their unknowns. In this problem, $3x+4 = x+5$ and $3x+2 = 2x+6$ are not equivalent. You could make the apple equation $3x+4 = x+5$ into a simpler story for younger kids by subtracting one unknown from both sides. The result is an equivalent equation, $2x+4 = 5$.

SAME TECHNIQUE - DIFFERENT PROBLEM

Compute the sum

1+2+3+4+...+98+99+100+99+98+...+3+2+1

Towards the solution

Here is Dr. T's favorite example of the power of a picture. Can you draw a picture that shows that 1+2+3+4+5+4+3+2+1 equals 5×5, which is 25?

STEPS TO SOLUTION

1. Have an emotional reaction to the problem. After all, it seems that you'll have to do a lot of arithmetic, groan! Unless it can be helped. Aha!

2. Wishful thinking: what if we only needed to add the first five numbers 1+2+3+4+5+4+3+2+1? Let's try that and see if we notice a pattern.

3. Draw. We frequently think of number symbols, forgetting that those symbols are just shortcuts. But sometimes it might be better to avoid the shortcut! What if we draw dots for each number? How can we draw them to make our job of adding up easier?

1+2+3+4+5+4+3+2+1 = 5×5 = 25

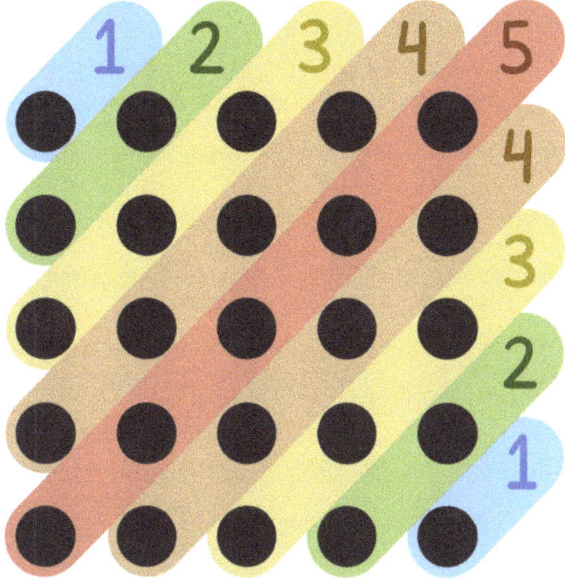

Back to the original problem. What is the sum 1+2+3+4+...+98+99+100+99 +98+...+3+2+1?

TECHNIQUE 5

MAKE IT SMALL

Some math problems you come across seem too big, too complicated, too much to take on. How do you eat a really huge cake? One bite at a time! That's realistic. But Technique 5 is stronger. It is like a superpower, because remaking the world is what mathematics is all about. Make the cake small: shrink it to fit your plate!

 ## DR. T'S PROBLEM

Arrange four pencils on the table so that each pencil touches each of the other three.

 ## STEPS TO SOLUTION

1. React emotionally to the problem. After experimenting a bit, does it seem impossible?

2. Make a wish: would this puzzle be easier to solve if there were fewer pencils?

2a. Make another wish: I wish pencils were bendy. Then I could easily connect them all to each other. Sure, why not! Let's explore how the object's properties affect the solution. We can try socks or laces. Maybe the problem would be easier to solve if pencils weren't so difficult to balance? Let's try using craft sticks instead. Explore as many "what ifs" as you and your child wants!

3. Make it small. Let's try to arrange two pencils so that each touches the other one. This is so easy that it sounds silly to describe.

   Let's build up from this and add a third pencil. Can we arrange three pencils so that they touch each other?

Yes! Let's get the fourth pencil. Hmm… Can we somehow use the answer for three pencils? Yes! We can lay the fourth pencil on top like this:

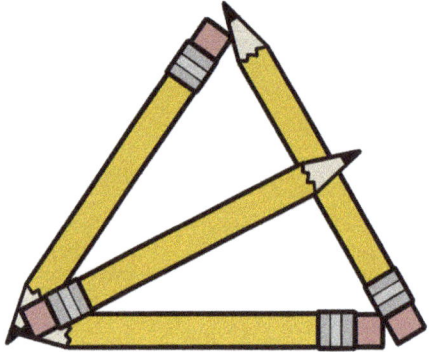

We are on a roll! Let's add another pencil. So now, with five pencils, can we arrange them so each touches all the other ones? Can we do it with six pencils? How about seven pencils?

I TRIED THIS TECHNIQUE AND…

Instead of figuring out a solution to the problem, my child wanted to build various patterns and shapes with the craft sticks. How can I keep my child on task?

You might need to pull out the craft sticks a few more times and let your child explore them in a way that is interesting to him. It helps with spatial reasoning in general! But at some point, your child will reach the stage when he is still interested in the sticks, but is running out of his own ideas about what to do with them. This is a perfect time to introduce the problem.

TODDLER TIME

For younger kids, use objects that are larger and less slippery than pencils, such as large carrots, hot dogs, or construction set bricks. Don't just say numbers, but show all numbers with quantities of objects.

Toddler Time Adaptations

- Use large objects and gross motor skills.
- Keep the numbers small.
- Use sets of objects to show numbers.

SCAVENGER HUNT

All complex occupations developed ways to shrink big projects into more manageable versions. For example, architects build "toy" models when they design. Cooks try new recipes with just one portion before using it at a big dinner. Artists make quick, small sketches to plan their paintings. Find more examples from your life or professions you're familiar with.

WHAT IS THE BIG IDEA HERE?

- **Networks** are formed by the pencils which are "nodes," and two nodes are linked when the two pencils touch.
- **Topology and configuration** are demonstrated as the physicality of the pencils puts restrictions on the networks that can be constructed.

SAME TECHNIQUE - DIFFERENT PROBLEM

Nine blocks are arranged in a 3×3 square grid. I want to remove three blocks so that when I look at the holes left behind, no row or column in the array contains more than one hole. In how many ways can this be done?

STEPS TO SOLUTION

1. Have an emotional reaction to the problem. Grrr, how can I ever count all possible configurations of holes?!

2. Draw a picture or build a model with actual blocks.

3. Make a wish. The problem would be easier if we had fewer blocks on a smaller grid or if we had to pick just one or two blocks at a time (or maybe not—try it and see!).

4. The problem is easy with 2×2 grids and combinations of two blocks. When you increase the size of the grid, it becomes harder to keep track of combinations. Use graph paper to draw all your past combinations.

Questions and Answers #2

Q: YOU SAY "REACT EMOTIONALLY," BUT WHAT IF MY REACTIONS ARE NEGATIVE? DOES IT MEAN I HATE MATH?

A: Whether a problem at first makes you feel anxious, apprehensive, uncertain, curious, impatient, glad, excited, or anything else, it's okay. It's normal to feel afraid or lost as your first reaction to a math problem. It doesn't mean you hate all math, or are bad at it. Go with the full range of emotions, and you will be able to experience the joy of working out a problem and exhilaration of mastering it. Don't be too afraid of your own fear. But if you feel overwhelmed, take a break.

Q: MY CHILD GETS EASILY DISCOURAGED IF SHE CAN'T SOLVE THE PROBLEM RIGHT AWAY. HOW CAN I HELP HER STAY MOTIVATED?

A: Explain that even professional mathematicians feel like your child does: stuck or frustrated over problems. But they have techniques to keep them going when the going gets tough:

- **Make yourselves comfortable** for a slow, relaxing activity without any hurry whatsoever. Prepare tasty snacks, put a purring kitty or a teddy bear in your lap, turn relaxing music on if you like that. Some children like to solve problems lying down or bouncing on exercise balls.
- Ask your child how long she thinks this problem "should" take. Tell her you are dedicating about twenty times more time so you can be at peace, and explore. Teach her the benefits of **giving oneself time** - it's the best insurance against anxiety.
- But you don't have to spend all that time all at once. **Take breaks** any time you want, but always discuss and schedule the next time

to go back to the problem. Sometimes children want to schedule it on another day, which gives them time to think and to calm the nerves. To keep the problem on your mind, put the materials where you can see them, in an activity basket or on your bulletin board.

- Assure your child by unlimited tech and human support. Explain she can **use many tools**, such as rulers for measuring, fingers for counting, or computers for modeling. Invite her to **ask you for any type and amount of help**. Sometimes she will ask you to show her how you would solve the problem beginning to end - do so! It's a form of learning. There are infinitely many problems in the world, so you won't run out. But do pause in your story, in case she wants to try the next step herself.

Q: MY CHILD STOPS WORKING ON A PROBLEM AS SOON AS ANOTHER CHILD COMES UP WITH A SOLUTION, EVEN IF INCORRECT. HOW CAN I HELP HIM STAY MOTIVATED?

A: **Offer problems that have many solutions or multiple ways to arrive at the same solution. Ask everyone in the group to offer several solutions or several ways to get to the same solution.** The child who comes up with a solution first will have to continue working, like everyone else, and your child will see that it makes sense to do so. Make it a habit to seek three to four answers to any question you ask.

Q: HOW DO I KEEP FROM GIVING AWAY TOO MUCH, OR ANSWERING TOO MANY QUESTIONS FOR THE CHILDREN?

A: When it comes to answering questions, become one of the children: take turns answering just like the rest of them. If you have six children in the group, you will be child #7 when it comes to answering questions. In general, **take turns** asking and answering.

Q: MY CHILD DOESN'T LIKE WRITING OR DRAWING. HOW CAN I MODIFY PROBLEMS TO MOVE AWAY FROM PEN AND PAPER?

A: Use a whiteboard. It is irresistible to most children. And if not, start by declaring that you shall be the "scribe" today, and will write on the board whatever your child asks you to write. You will likely not describe or draw exactly what the child has in mind. Often children will want to come up and correct what you have scribed.

Pretend-play problems with toys or household objects. Model with construction sets. You can even build out of pens and paper! Make your child a character in the math story, and use the whole body to show movement, angles, or reflections.

Q: WHAT IF I CAN'T SOLVE THE PROBLEM AFTER ALL THE EXPLORATION?

A: You will model an extremely valuable math lesson for your children. Some problems resist our efforts for a while. This experience is true to how math and science work. Take a break, come to our Ask and Tell forum for a discussion with colleagues, and then attack the problem again. That's what math people do with their problems!

Q: MY CHILD GETS VERY FRUSTRATED WITH THESE PROBLEMS. HE LIKES TO LISTEN TO STORIES AND IS OFTEN EAGER TO TRY TO SOLVE PRESENTED PROBLEMS. BUT VERY OFTEN HE ENDS UP IN TEARS. WHAT CAN I DO TO HELP?

A: Observe what makes your child go from joy to tears. Investigate. Does it have to do with objects (joy) vs. words and symbols (frustration)? Or is it algebra (joy) vs. geometry (frustration)? Or is it the difficulty level?

A lot of the techniques we discuss in other questions, such as seeking math excitement, will help. But what you describe is beyond discouragement: it's an acute stress! What to do?

- First of all, stop. **Never, ever do novel math with a distressed child**. Emotional upset turns off higher brain functions you need for problem-solving, and disrupts memory. That's why people in high-stress professions, such as firefighters, train and train on simple moves, until they become beyond automatic.

- Later, when the child is calm and happy, discuss plans for mathematical well-being. Invite your child to **make a list called *Wonderful Things*** that make him feel calm and focused. Write, draw, or photograph the results of that brainstorm: food, pets, toys, being outdoors, music, new markers, sitting on an exercise ball - these are ideas many kids bring up. You can suggest ideas too, such as massage, meditation, or reciting something familiar. Maybe you will solve problems while massaging your son's shoulders, with snacks on the table, using his favorite action figures for prompts.

- Agree on a code word or draw a big PAUSE button on paper. Whenever your child uses that word or "presses" the button, take a break. At first, kids will do that all the time, to test that it really works. Just bear with it. Your kid must firmly believe in his power to stop when going forward would hurt too much.

Q: HOW CAN I SUGGEST A WAY TOWARD A SOLUTION WITHOUT GIVING AWAY TOO MUCH OF AN ANSWER? ASKING OPEN-ENDED QUESTIONS IS HARDER THAN IT SOUNDS.

A: This is indeed a delicate and subtle art! One trouble with the dynamic of a classroom-like setup is that everyone knows that the "teacher" already knows the answer and is just pretending not to. If you offer an open-ended problem, but children stall and expect you to lead, talk about the psychology of it all. "Do you think I, as the grown-up, already know the answer?" See where that conversation goes. Then propose the challenge to come up with a variation of the question that nobody in the room knows the answer to. Even with the very young, be absolutely upfront about issues likes these.

To nudge a stuck activity in the right direction without giving away the answer, you can always ask: "Have we tried all the problem-solving approaches?" List some, and invite children to see if a strategy might possibly apply. Or appeal to past discussion: "Have we tried every idea that has already been mentioned today in this room? Didn't Chris say something about it?"

Q: I READ THROUGH THE STEPS TO SOLVING A PROBLEM AND, ALTHOUGH I SEE WHAT IS BEING DONE, I DON'T UNDERSTAND WHY IT IS DONE THIS WAY AND WHY IT WORKS THE WAY IT WORKS. SHOULD I SKIP PRESENTING THIS PROBLEM TO MY CHILD?

A: Bring this very issue to your child! Try presenting this problem and saying: "I need your help with this one. Here's the question. Any thoughts on how to solve it?" Your child may naturally generate ideas that start a path to thinking about answering the problem. If so, follow that conversation!

Or your child may be "stuck" too. In this case, describe or model with objects the solution that you read. Discuss your thoughts on that solution, in particular, that you can't see why this solution is working the way it does. If understanding does not emerge in the modeling and discussion, ask other local people, or post your question on the forum. When in doubt about an issue, make it a shared conversation with your child, your friends, and your colleagues online.

TECHNIQUE 6

ELIMINATE INCORRECT CHOICES

Would you like to know a fool-proof strategy for always getting a correct answer to a multiple-choice question? Here it is: eliminate incorrect choices! It sounds like teasing, but this is a real problem-solving technique. Oh, and since this is not a test, take as long as you need to think about your options. If you and your child enjoy the problems in this chapter, search for Knights and Knaves puzzles, Four Card puzzles, and other lateral thinking problems.

DR. T'S PROBLEM

A teacher draws horses on a sheet of paper and holds the sheet up to the class. She asks Lashana, "How many horses do you see altogether?" Lashana replies, "THREE." The teacher says, "Correct!" She then asks Juan how many horses he sees. He replies, "FOUR" and the teacher responds, "Correct!"

How many horses did the teacher draw on the paper, given that both Lashana and Juan were indeed correct with their answers?

(A) Fewer than three horses

(B) Three horses

(C) Four horses

(D) Seven horses

STEPS TO SOLUTION

1. React emotionally to the problem.

2. Eliminate incorrect choices. If the teacher drew fewer than three horses, neither Lashana nor Juan could possibly be correct. If the teacher drew just three horses, Juan cannot be correct with his answer. And if the teacher drew four, Lashana could not be correct (unless the teacher covered one with her hand when she asked Lashana!).

So the answer has to be option (D). How is that possible?

Hint: A sheet of paper has two sides!

I TRIED THIS TECHNIQUE AND...

My child came up with some very creative solutions, but none of them is the solution in the book. What should I do?

Do these solutions work? That is, do they make sense to you? If yes, then accept them and acknowledge the creativity. Then use them as conversation starters: which of these working solutions do you like personally and why? Some mathematicians like their solutions to be elegant and short. Others prefer surprising solutions. Yet others like more predictable solutions, because they are easier to explain. If the solution does not work for you, tweak it until it does, and offer your version to the child. You can collect many versions over time, especially if you offer the problem to family and friends.

 ## TODDLER TIME

Toddlers may not be troubled by the fact Lashana and Juan see different correct things at once. Some children as old as five or six completely miss the punch line of this puzzle, because their concept of "correct" is very different from that of grown-ups.

For very young kids, use smaller numbers. Lashana's reply might be "One horse," Juan's might be "Two horses," and the possible answer choices would be:

  (A) No horses
  (B) One horse
  (C) Two horses
  (D) Three horses

Young children might talk about the paper changing between questions, or Juan counting make-believe horses, and other fantasy solutions. Support these and all other discussions, because they give you more chances to use number and logic words in ways meaningful to each child. Always support and celebrate fantasy, but gently help kids to separate it from the reality. When discussing the reality, eliminate choices that are not possible in this world.

Toddler Time Adaptations

- Keep the numbers small.
- Use sets of objects to show numbers.
- Tell a story of what's going on in the problem, and why.

SCAVENGER HUNT

Eliminating wrong choices is a staple of deduction. Older kids will enjoy this technique in *Sherlock Holmes* and other detective stories. For younger kids, there are books with the theme of eliminating hilarious options that don't work. In *Where's My Cow?*, the character asks: "Is this my cow? It goes, 'Hruuugh!' It is a hippopotamus! That's not my cow!" In *Green Eggs and Ham*, Sam offers a lot of ways to eat that get rejected (until finally, the option "to try" instead of "to eat" works):

> I would not, could not, in the rain.
> Not in the dark. Not on a train,
> Not in a car, Not in a tree.
> I do not like them, Sam, you see.
> Not in a house. Not in a box.
> Not with a mouse. Not with a fox.

WHAT IS THE BIG IDEA HERE?

- **Deductive reasoning** is a step-by-step method for logically reaching certain conclusions from statements.
- **Lateral thinking** is the method of solving problems through systematic and holistic creative insight. The problem of horses

requires deductive reasoning to eliminate incorrect choices, and lateral thinking to figure out how the correct choice can possibly work.

SAME TECHNIQUE - DIFFERENT PROBLEM

Read the following three sentences:

1. Exactly one of these sentences is FALSE.
2. Exactly two of these sentences are FALSE.
3. All three of these sentences are FALSE.

For each of these three sentences, determine whether it is true or false.

STEPS TO SOLUTION

1. Have an emotional reaction to the problem.

2. Eliminate incorrect choices. The last sentence cannot be true because if it were, it would also say that it is false. Oops! So the last sentence is FALSE. Can it be the only false sentence? That is, can it be false and the other two sentences true?

TECHNIQUE 7

PERSEVERANCE IS KEY

Perseverance: finishing what you started regardless of the obstacles that stand in the way.

– Urban Dictionary

 ## DR. T'S PROBLEM

This puzzle also appears in Without Words by James Tanton, Tarquin Press, 2015.

The setup:

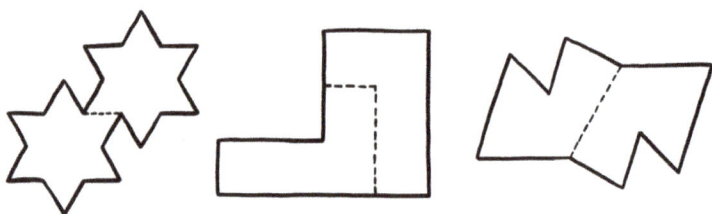

The question:

STEPS TO SOLUTION

1. React emotionally to the problem.

2. Remember: perseverance is key!

3. Do something. The biggest help for kids solving these puzzles is suggesting they make some of their own! When children make puzzles, they notice helpful spatial patterns and properties. Here's how:

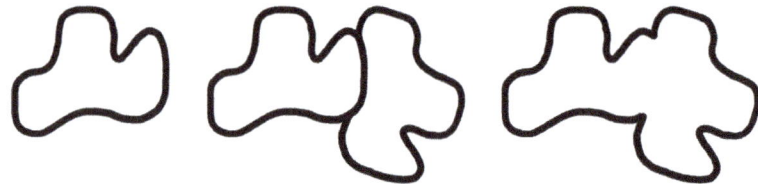

Step 1: Fold paper in two and draw a shape.
Step 2: Cut it out, through both layers, so you have two copies.
Step 3: Rotate one of the copies, until you like how the copies fit together.
Step 4: Trace the whole thing. Voila! A puzzle!

I TRIED THIS TECHNIQUE AND...

I felt frustrated. My child did not approach this problem in a systematic way and ignored my suggestions. As a result, he spent a lot of time repeatedly making the same mistake, trying the same combinations and did not solve the problem. What should I do?

What you do depends on whether your child also felt frustrated. When children play ball, they can miss the hoop hundreds of times and yet feel great. Healthy free play is not systematic, so don't try to turn math play into a training exercise. If you can join as a playmate, do so, but don't try to coach - yet! The time for a suggestion or two comes only when children are done with free play, or when they get frustrated.

TODDLER TIME

Toddlers may enjoy these puzzles once they understand what to do. Start with shapes that resemble something; for example, a lizard or a favorite toy.

Try shapes that have three parts instead of two, like the Isle of Man flag. The repetition of three parts is easier to see.

Make puzzles together with your child. Ask if your child would make a puzzle for you to solve.

You may need to show an example or two of such puzzles each day for several days, before the activity clicks. Likewise, some babies spit out a new food many times before they start eating it. Persevere!

Toddler Time Adaptations

- Pretend-play with characters that matter to your child.
- Make and remix puzzles together with the child.

SCAVENGER HUNT

Deconstruct the objects that made shadows by looking at the shadow. For example, reverse-engineer hand positions from looking at shadow puppets. Look at creatures from myth, fantasy, or science-fiction. What parts went into making of a pegasus, a sphynx, or a mermaid?

WHAT IS THE BIG IDEA HERE?

- **Isometry** is a transformation that keeps all the lengths and the angles in a shape the same. "Iso" means sameness and "metry" means measurement. All pieces in the puzzles are isometries of one another by **rotations**, **reflections**, or **glides**. It's pretty easy to rotate or to mirror a shape. But the perplexity of the puzzles is figuring out which shapes and which transformations have been applied!

SAME TECHNIQUE - DIFFERENT PROBLEM

Find a square number whose final digit is 8.

STEPS TO SOLUTION

1. React emotionally to the problem.

2. Do something. First, you may need to explore square numbers with your child. Kids who like to play with numbers but can't multiply fluently can use a spreadsheet to compute. You can also find the first few square numbers by making square arrays out of raisins, coins, or other counters. Here are the first few numbers and their squares:

0	1	2	3	4	5	6	7	8	9	10
0	1	4	9	16	25	36	49	64	81	100

Hmm. None of those end in 8.

3.   Make a wish. If we keep hunting for a while, it seems a long way off before we find one that does end in 8. If only there was a more systematic way of working toward the solution.

Do you notice any patterns in the end digits of squares? For example:

If our number ends with 0, then so will its square. No good!

If our number ends with 1, then so will its square. No good!

Looks like end digits of numbers are important for end digits of their squares. Let's persevere! Are there more patterns?

If our number ends with 2, what happens to its square? Can its square end with 8? Experiment with as many numbers as your child wants to try:

2	12	22	72	992
4	144	484	5184	984064

If our number ends with 2, then its square always ends in 4.

No good! If our number ends in 3...

4.   Keep going! Perseverance is key!

SECOND-GUESS THE AUTHOR

> *- Knock-knock!*
> *- Who's there?*
> *- Doughnut!*

Before you ask, "Doughnut who?", think of why the joke teller chose a doughnut over all other pastries. Do not tell the others, because second-guessing a joke teller won't make you popular at parties. But it is another powerful tool for your and your child's problem-solving tool belts.

DR. T'S PROBLEM

This puzzle also appears in Without Words by James Tanton, Tarquin Press, 2015.

The set up...

The question...

Another question...

STEPS TO SOLUTION

1. React emotionally to the problem. What do these confusing squiggles even mean?

2. Do something. How about we just color the pictures and get the answer that way? Okay, it'll be pretty easy with the first puzzle. The second one is a bit more tedious. The third one might take a while, unless...

3. Second-guess the author. ...Unless there's an easier way to work it out, without coloring. Hmm, was there a reason the author showed us the colored-in puzzles?

Hint: Think of a picture as an island in a lake on an island...

I TRIED THIS TECHNIQUE AND...

I ended up second-guessing myself. It always happens without answer keys in the back of the book. Did my kid and I solve the problem correctly? Did I even understand what is required in this problem? How can I check myself on the problems when no answer is provided?

This is a big question, because methods of checking depend on the type of problem. When in doubt, ask a friend or post your solution online and ask others what they think. This is exactly what mathematicians do! Teach your kid to discuss problems with friends, and to use friendly online forums where other students discuss problems.

You can also test any general method you develop by using it to solve smaller and simpler versions of the same problem. For example, some might solve the puzzle by drawing a line from outside the region to the given dot, and then tracing their finger along the line: they note the boundary crossings from water to land and from land to water, as they do. Does that technique work for the three simpler examples at the start of the puzzle? Does it work for a single circular island? A single circular island with a lake in it? (And add the results of these tests when you discuss your solution with a friend or online!)

 ## TODDLER TIME

Drawing islands is easy enough for a toddler to do. It is great for pretend-play and stories. Where should we gather coconuts? And where should we go fish? If we start outside in the water and cross an edge, we step onto land. Coconuts grow on land. "Walk" a little toy character across drawings, or make puzzles big enough for the kids to walk them!

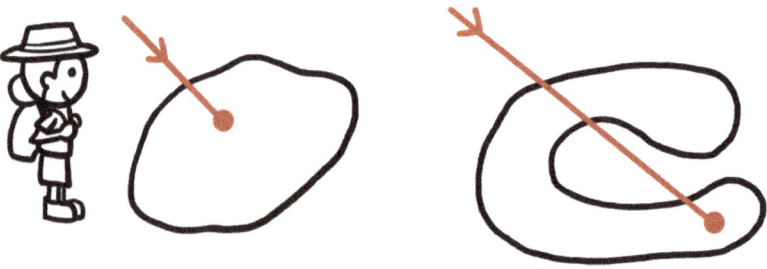

For a more complicated island starting out in the water and moving along to a given point, each time we cross an edge we *switch*: from water to land, or from land to water.

Toddler Time Adaptations

- Use large objects and gross motor skills.
- Pretend-play with characters that matter to your child.
- Tell a story of what's going on in the problem and why.
- Make and remix puzzles together with the child.

 ## SCAVENGER HUNT

Open Google Earth and put your math goggles on. Look for an island in a lake on an island in a lake. As you travel around the globe, make sure to explore Philippines, Sumatra, and Canada for some amazing island-in-a-lake-on-an-island views.

 ## WHAT IS THE BIG IDEA HERE?

- **Topology** studies insides, outsides, and loops within shapes, rather than particular forms and sizes.
- **Parity** says whether a number is even or odd, a lamp bulb is on or off, a cog is turning clockwise or counter-clockwise, and so on. The parity of switches between water and land is the key to this puzzle.

SAME TECHNIQUE - DIFFERENT PROBLEM

Lulu was multiplying two positive integers. Let's call them A and B. The number A has two digits. In doing her multiplication Lulu accidentally reversed the digits of A and she got erroneous answer 65. What is the correct value of the product of A and B?

STEPS TO SOLUTION

1. React emotionally to the problem. Do I have to try all two-digit numbers to find A?!

2. Second-guess the author: why the number 65 in this puzzle? It must have been chosen for a reason. 65 is a product of 5 and 13, and these two numbers only. There are no other possibilities, like there would be with 64 (2 and 32, or 4 and 16). So...

TECHNIQUE 9

AVOID HARD WORK

Folk wisdom can be confusing. We are told "Hard work pays off," and at the same time, "Work smart, not hard." Technique 9 focuses on the second saying. To apply it to Dr.T's problem, use these nuggets of wisdom: "A picture is worth a thousand words," and "The more things change, the more they stay the same."

 ## DR. T'S PROBLEM

Here is an L-shaped piece.

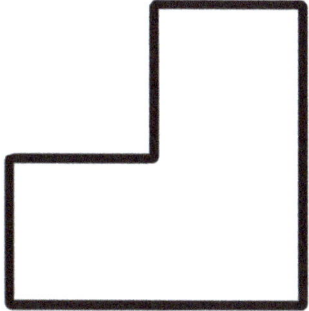

We can cut it into two identical pieces, or three identical pieces, or four identical pieces.

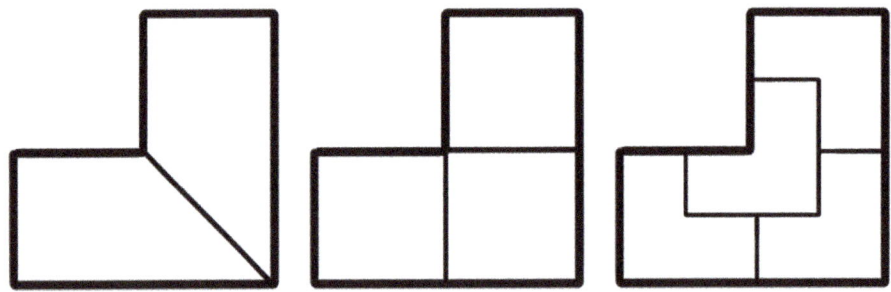

How could you chop the L-shaped piece into 300 identical pieces?

STEPS TO SOLUTION

1. React emotionally to the problem. There is no way I want to draw three hundred pieces!

2. Avoid hard work. Could I use one of the above pictures to imagine an answer to the question, instead of drawing?

    Hint 1: use the picture of an L-shaped block chopped into 3 pieces, because 300 = 3×100. Aha!

    Hint 2: how would you go about dividing the L shape into 8 equal pieces? Or 10 equal pieces?

    Hint 3: "The more things change, the more they stay the same": mathematics is about similarities of different things. Notice what stays the same as you divide the shape in different ways.

I drew the puzzle, but the kids weren't interested in systematic solutions. They drew lots of colorful lines and we ended up with a fun-looking grid of sorts, but that was it. What did I do wrong and how to get the kids back on track?

"If at first you don't succeed, try and try again." I promise, this is the last folk saying in the chapter! Kids often need a break after the first round of free play with the problem. Keep the fun-looking grid where kids can see it on your fridge or a bulletin board. In a day or two, ask the question again: "I wonder if this time we can cut the shape into fair, equal pieces. Let's try!" Sometimes kids are inspired to try again if you tell them a new story, or use a different material, such as playdough or colored paper.

TODDLER TIME

As you tell this story, play it out with toys. Pay attention to things that stay the same throughout the story.

Little Linda had a birthday. Her cake was shaped like the letter "L" for Linda. Linda and the two friends she invited to a party all wanted cake. But they also wanted their pieces to be exactly the same! So the cake had to be cut into three pieces.

Linda and her friends had little brothers who came over at cake time. Can the girls share the cake with their brothers? What if each girl had two little brothers who came over? What if three more friends showed up?

What if Linda and her two friends each had a hundred friends?!
(Expect kids to laugh, and to draw "many-many-many" lines to show a hundred pieces.)

Toddler Time Techniques Used

- Use large objects and gross motor skills.
- Use sets of objects to show numbers.
- Pretend-play with characters that matter to your child.
- Tell a story of what's going on in the problem and why.

SCAVENGER HUNT

The number of friends at Linda's birthday party changes: it is a variable. But no matter how many friends show up - two, three, or three hundred - you use a similar idea to solve the problem. Look for more situations where the numbers or measures vary, but the overall situation stays the same. For example, you probably fold sheets, towels, and pillowcases in two, until they fit on your shelf, but the number of folds varies. You turn on the same water faucet to fill in a glass, a pot, or a bucket; the time it takes varies. Every birthday, you add one year to your age, whatever it is.

WHAT IS THE BIG IDEA HERE?

- **Iteration** is using the same technique again and again, however many times you need to.
- **Variable** is a quantity or measure that changes while the pattern stays the same.
- **Congruence** refers to shapes of the same size and structure which are placed differently. One can place one congruent figure on top of another, matching all the edges and angles.

SAME TECHNIQUE - DIFFERENT PROBLEM

What is the sum of the first 100 odd numbers?

STEPS TO SOLUTION

1. React emotionally to the problem. There's no way I want to add "one plus three plus five plus seven plus..."

2. Avoid hard work. Let's look for an easier approach. Let's get a feel for matters. The sum of the first two odd numbers is:

   1+3 = 4

   The sum of the first three odd numbers is:

   1+3+5 = 9

   The sum of the first four odd numbers is:

   1+3+5+7 = 16

   Hmm! The results are very special numbers...

TECHNIQUE 10

GO TO THE XTREMES

Let's play a word associations game. What comes to mind when you hear the word **extreme**? Is it weather, sports, coupon-clipping, or adventure? How about math? It helps to ponder extreme versions of your problems. Once you master this technique, you will feel as if you've gained an extra power, a mathematical X-gene.

 ## DR. T'S PROBLEM

Each morning on my way to work from the subway, I walk up the moving escalator as fast as I can. I count 20 steps each time.

If I walked up slowly, would I count more steps or fewer steps?

If I ran up even more quickly than I usually do, would I count more steps or fewer steps?

STEPS TO SOLUTION

1. React emotionally to the problem.

2. Go to the Xtremes. What is the slowest I can walk on a escalator? If I walked up the escalator at this extremely slow speed, how many steps would I count?

I TRIED THIS TECHNIQUE AND...

I kept thinking, but what if it's an impossible-to-solve problem?

You should add "Is it possible?" at the start of every problem! It's easy to forget that not all problems have solutions. This is a wonderful "teachable moment" for both kids and adults; not all problems have solutions, adults don't always possess solutions, and some problems have more than one solution. Make it a habit to give kids some impossible tasks and unsolvable problems, such as, "Can you figure out how to bite your elbow?" or "How do you cut a square into three equal squares?" But be prepared to accept creative, out-of-the box solutions!

TODDLER TIME

Be prepared to take your youngster to the nearest escalator for some hands-on (or rather, feet-on) exploration. Walk up, count stairs. Walk up slower, count stairs. Walk up faster, count stairs. As with all stairs, be careful about slipping or bumping into other people.

Toddler Time Adaptations

- Use large objects and gross motor skills.
- Keep the numbers small.

SCAVENGER HUNT

Zero often makes young kids laugh: "I hold zero elephants in my hand!" For jolly times, hunt for zero and other extremes, such as an army of one, infinite and zero slopes, or the straight angle.

WHAT IS THE BIG IDEA HERE?

- **Extreme value** is the minimum or maximum possible value of a variable.
- **Variable** is a quantity or measure that changes while the pattern stays the same.

SAME TECHNIQUE - DIFFERENT PROBLEM

Is it possible to write six different digits on a page so that no two of them add up to 10?

If your kid likes addition, try this version: Is it possible to write fifty-one different two-digit numbers on a page so that no two of them sum to 100? The steps to the solution are similar.

STEPS TO SOLUTION

1. React emotionally to the problem. There are lots of possible combinations of six digits!

2. Go to the Xtremes. How many digits are there? 0 to 9, so ten in all. Let's ask something absurd. Is it possible to write a million different one-digit numbers on a page, so that no two of them add up to 10? No! There are only ten different ones!

3. Slightly less absurd then: is it possible to write all ten digits on a page so that no two of them add up to 10? No! You'll have problematic pairs, like 9 and 1.

Oooh! This reveals that we need to avoid the pairs 9 and 1, 8 and 2, etc. We can have one and only one digit from each pair. How many pairs, that is, how many digits to throw away? How many are left?

Questions and Answers #3

Q: HOW DO I MAKE SURE THAT MY CHILD HAS LEARNED OR UNDERSTOOD THE PROBLEM-SOLVING TECHNIQUES?

A: Even if you worked on problem-solving in the context of number patterns, you can't just ask "What is 1+2-3+4?" and use the correctness or incorrectness of their answer to judge your teaching success. Problem-solving is a type of fluid cognition, which you can't test just by correctness of answers. Instead, **look for your child using practices and techniques for new problems**. If your child experiments more, asks about extreme cases of situations, or second-guesses you when you ask questions, you will know that these techniques have sunk in. You may want to print out the ten techniques so you remember to apply them in your day-to-day life!

Q: EXPLORATION SOUNDS GREAT, BUT I WOULD LIKE TO TRACK MY CHILD'S PROGRESS. HOW CAN I DO IT?

A: **Reflect on learning after the activities**. Keep a journal of what you notice, or write to your friends online. You can reflect on the ten problem-solving techniques, and make your own list of other techniques you notice. You can video-record your child telling you something about activities, because many children love to be on camera. Ask your child to pose for a photo with the math notes or objects. "Smile - it's math!" Put the photos where the child can see, so you can reflect and build on past activities together.

Q: WHY CAN'T I JUST SHOW MY CHILD EXACTLY WHAT TO DO AND ASK HER TO FOLLOW THE EXAMPLE?

A: **Because you can't get there from here**. Problem-solving is as different from the exercise of following examples as hiking through unexplored wilderness is from driving your car on a highway. Yes, in both cases you see some scenery. But you need different gear, different skills, and very different dispositions. Both problem-solving and exercises are useful, but you can't learn one from doing the other.

In problem-solving you want to teach your child the confidence to try new ideas, to explore possibilities, to not be afraid to follow different paths and see where they might go, but to feel at ease to change paths if that route doesn't look fruitful - basically, to have the ease and confidence of mind to make judgment calls about the state of one's reasoning. In problem-solving we teach self-assured thinking, which embraces the art of joyful flailing, self-assessing that flailing, and pinpointing the keys that lead to success within it. The solutions to interesting and meaningful problems in life often aren't procedural. One needs the confidence to stretch one's thinking, even to begin to figure out how one might start to approach them!

Q: HOW DO I CHECK WHETHER MY CHILD UNDERSTANDS WHY THE SOLUTION WORKS INSTEAD OF JUST FOLLOWING THE EXAMPLE?

A: The fun part of problem-solving is that **you get to *own* the problem, and can therefore change it and mess with it in any way you like**. Doing so tests understanding. For example, ask questions about possible changes:

- Was the number 5 important in this question? Could we do this with a different number?
- Does it matter that this piece turned clockwise? Would the answer change if it turned the other way?
- Can we make up a variation of this problem that works in the same way?

Children exercise their mathematical power and autonomy when they change problems. It feels satisfying to them, it helps them learn, and it gives you a window into their learning.

An Afterword from Dr. T

Good puzzles abound! And good puzzles re-emerge over and over again in all sorts of variations and contexts over the decades and over the centuries.

The cogs in Technique 1 serve as an example. Because they illustrate the notion of parity so beautifully, and because their relative speeds of turning depend on their numbers of teeth, cogs and gears have been a lovely source for activities in number theory since their invention. Search for "mathematics" and "gears" or "cogs" on the web to see many examples. Arranging dolls head to toe in a loop is really a simpler variation of a cog puzzle with cogs arranged in a loop: each change of doll orientation corresponds to moving to an adjacent cog and we thus need an even number of cogs.

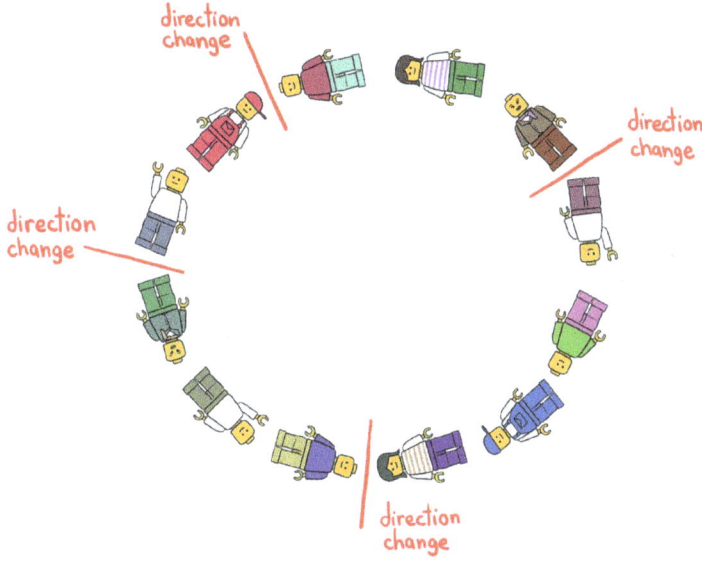

The idea of parity has been a favorite tool for puzzlists and mathematicians alike for centuries. The land and water puzzle in Technique 8 is a geometric manifestation of parity. Puzzles about sums or sets of consecutive integers, such as the library book puzzle in Technique 1, often involve parity:

- *Can you make change for a dollar using a combination of fifteen pennies, nickels, and quarters?*
- No. Fifteen odd amounts cannot sum to an even one-hundred.
- *Is 1000 the sum of six consecutive numbers?*
- No. The sum of three even and three odd numbers won't be an even thousand.

The scholars of ancient Greece often used geometric pictures of dots arranged in patterns to discover astounding results about arithmetic sums, as you are invited to do in Technique 9. The sums of the numbers from 1 to 5 and back down again, and the sum of the first five odd numbers, can both be seen in the picture of a five-by-five array of dots, for example.

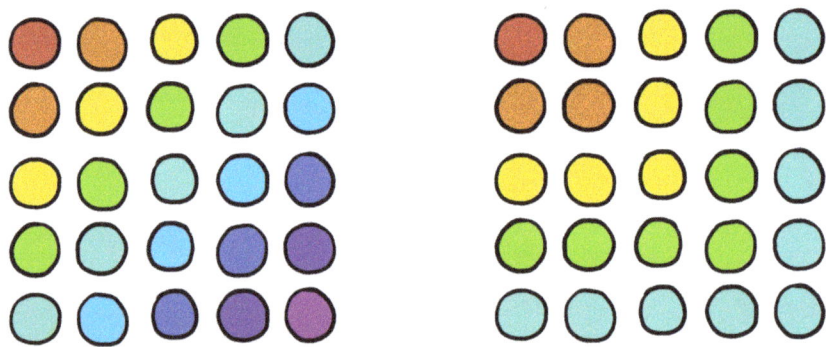

Finding patterns in mathematics is an art form, and explaining why those patterns work is often a deliciously hard challenge! In Technique 2, we saw that the final digits of the powers of two cycle through the list 2, 4, 8, and 6. *Why?* Pattern-based explorations also come from "*What if?...*" questions. What about the first digits of powers of two? Is there a power of two that begins with a seven?

Cutting shapes into pieces is a popular theme in recreational mathematics. Martin Gardner's book, *Aha! Gotcha; Aha! Insight,* has a lovely introduction to this topic. The cake puzzle from Technique 9 is inspired by Gardner's puzzles.

Some puzzles, such as those featuring stacking pencils in Technique 5, arranging sheep in Technique 3, and true/false statements in Technique 6, are simply classic. I personally don't know the origin of these puzzles, but I remember knowing them way back during my childhood! Other puzzles come from curricula; for instance, scales and balances in Technique 4 are often used to motivate beginning algebra students. The MAA collection of American Mathematical Competitions (maa.org/ci) has a whole host of engaging problems. The multiplication puzzle in Technique 8 was inspired by a competition problem.

Now that you are on the lookout for puzzles, you will no doubt come across more and more. As you do, you will begin to see connections between puzzles that, at first sight, seem very different. Your youngsters will too. And the more you play with puzzles, the more you will see how to create your own variations of them, along with brand new puzzles to share with the world! Enjoy being a mathematician!

Also Available:

Playing With Math

You and your children can play with mathematics! Learn how with more than thirty authors who share their math enthusiasm with their communities, families, and students. A different puzzle, game, or activity follows each chapter to help you get started.

Camp Logic

This is a book for teachers, parents, math circle leaders, and anyone who nurtures the intellectual development of children. You don't need any mathematical background at all to use these activities – all you need is a willingness to dig in and work toward solving problems, even when no obvious path to a solution presents itself. The games and activities in this book give students an informal, playful introduction to the very nature of mathematics and its underlying structure.

Available at NaturalMath.com and online book stores.
Published by Delta Stream Media, an imprint of Natural Math.
Make math your own, to make your own math!

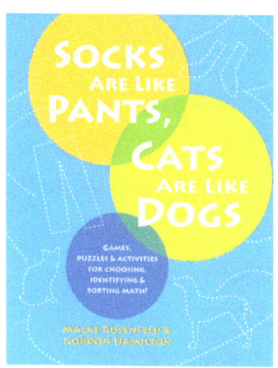

Socks Are Like Pants, Cats Are Like Dogs

Do you want your children to feel that algebra is beautiful, playful, and intuitive? Come play, solve, talk, and make math with us! This book is filled with a diverse collection of math games, puzzles, and activities exploring the mathematics of choosing, identifying and sorting.

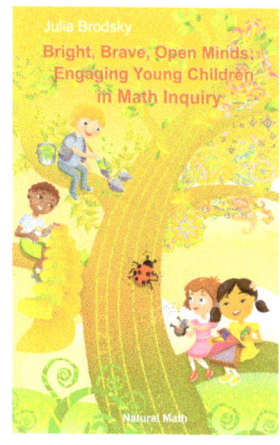

Bright, Brave, Open Minds

Teach problem-solving and spark curiosity! Explore with your own children or students as you drop your own predictions and allow the children to use their tastes and ideas as a rudder. This book introduces the beginning skills of problem solving to both children and the adults who teach them.

Available at NaturalMath.com and online book stores.
Published by Delta Stream Media, an imprint of Natural Math.
Make math your own, to make your own math!

Moebius Noodles

How do you want your child to feel about math? Confident, curious and deeply connected? Then Moebius Noodles is for you. It offers advanced math activities to fit your child's personality, interests, and needs. Learn how you can create an immersive rich math environment for your baby. Find out ways to help your toddler discover deep math in everyday experiences. Play games that will develop your child's sense of happy familiarity with mathematics. A five-year-old once asked us, "Who makes math?" and jumped for joy at the answer, "You!" Moebius Noodles helps you take small, immediate steps toward the sense of mathematical power. You and your child can make math your own. Together, make your own math!

Available at NaturalMath.com and online book stores.
Published by Delta Stream Media, an imprint of Natural Math.
Make math your own, to make your own math!

CPSIA information can be obtained
at www.ICGtesting.com
Printed in the USA
JSHW030237180920
7997JS00001B/2